Latimer Briefing 21

I0201176

THE CHURCH'S ONE FOUNDATION

WHAT ORTHODOXY IS AND WHY IT MATTERS

GERALD BRAY

The Latimer Trust

The Church's One Foundation: What orthodoxy Is and Why
It Matters
© Gerald Bray 2024. All rights reserved.
ISBN 978-1-916834-02-6
Cover image: Canva.
Published by the Latimer Trust, January 2024.

Scripture quotations are taken from The Holy Bible, English
Standard Version Copyright © 2001 by Crossway Bibles, a division
of Good News Publishers.

The Latimer Trust (formerly Latimer House, Oxford) is a
conservative evangelical research organisation within the Church
of England, whose main aim is to promote the history and theology
of Anglicanism as understood by those in the Reformed tradition.
Interested readers are welcome to consult its website for further
details of its many activities.

The Latimer Trust
London N14 4PS UK
Registered Charity: 1084337
Company Number: 4104465
www.latimertrust.org
administrator@latimertrust.org

CONTENTS

Foreword

As Gerald Bray notes, the concept of 'orthodoxy' has become more widespread in Christian vocabulary recently. Yet there is much confusion as to what it is and what it is not. Gerald has written this measured, forthright and informative briefing in order to dispel the confusion that surrounds the use of this word.

However, this is not a narrow discussion of terminology, it is in fact an exposition of the heart and core of the Christian faith. As we follow Jesus it is easy for us to get caught up in arguments and discussions about what is not so important. The great virtue of this work is that we are given a sure guide to what really matters. It helps us see the wood for the trees and thus equips us to work with all those who share a commitment to orthodoxy. It is this perspective which enables us to see the profound contradiction in the use of the term 'generous orthodoxy'.

Gerald's starting point is quite properly located in 2 Tim 1:13–14 where Paul speaks of 'the pattern of sound words'. The word 'orthodox' does not appear in the Bible but the concept is fundamental as this reference shows. The pages of this work are packed with relevant Bible references but in some sense the inspiration for its contents can be seen as coming from various hymns, and 'The Church's One Foundation' by S J Stone in particular. This might seem eccentric at first sight, but in fact there is good reason for this. Hymns that have stood the test of time are expressions of orthodox faith and life.

Those who have been familiar with Gerald's editorials in *Churchman* (now *Global Anglican*) will recognise the pithy style we find here. He has a remarkable capacity to bring clarity to complex issues and shed new light upon them. There is much here that comments on current circumstances within the Church of England, but these comments are not unfair or ill-considered. For example, the contempt by the revisionist minority for the majority of Anglicans and for due process is noted. All who follow Jesus in the Church of England and the wider Anglican world will benefit from reading this booklet.

In response to those who argue that the Creeds say nothing about heterosexual marriage we are reminded that even though the Creeds are very important they are incomplete expressions of an underlying orthodoxy. In reality it would be easier for the Church to permit polygamy than to bless same-sex marriage.

We also read that between right and wrong there is no such thing as 'good disagreement', that the practice of orthodoxy is vital, and that we must take Jesus as he is given to us. The Bible's perspective on revisionists who have known the way of truth is underlined, as is the godly way of responding to provocations from that quarter.

Personally I found the later sections which deal with prayer and spiritual warfare particularly encouraging. We often neglect the resources the Lord gives us for living out our orthodoxy. To this end, the mini-exposition of Ephesians 6 is most rewarding. These resources are precious because they are not available to those who have departed from orthodoxy.

Do sit down and read this booklet carefully. It will remind you of what is really important in following Jesus. It will remind you that this concept of orthodoxy matters because it is the pathway to life. It will remind you also that (as Gerald says) orthodoxy is not a majority faith.

Mark Burkill
Chairman of the Latimer Trust

1. What Is Orthodoxy?

Recent controversies in the Church of England, and in the wider Anglican world, have led to a renewed interest in what is being increasingly called 'orthodoxy'. We are used to labels like 'conservative', 'traditional', 'mainstream', 'evangelical' and 'catholic', but 'orthodoxy', though it is by no means a new concept, strikes many people as unfamiliar, at least in an Anglican context. What does it mean? Can it be defined? Given the situation that we are in at present, it is unlikely that any definition will satisfy everybody. Some will see no need for it, others will eschew all labels as inadequate, misleading, and perhaps even ungodly. Still others will claim to be 'orthodox' in their own eyes and resent the fact that they are not generally recognised as such by others. The danger for anyone foolhardy enough to try to pin the term down is that critics will read any explanation of it as self-justifying – this is what the author thinks, they will say, and he is trying to divide the Church into those who agree with him (his fellow 'orthodox') and those who do not. As with all things Anglican, difficulties and disagreements abound, but whether we like it or not, the concept of 'orthodoxy' has re-entered our ecclesiastical vocabulary and some attempt must be made to determine what it is – and what it is not.

Why are the more familiar labels not adequate enough to describe 'orthodoxy' accurately? For example, most Anglicans who self-identify as orthodox would probably accept that they are in some sense 'conservative'. But 'conservative' is a vague term that can mean many different things. It often implies social and/or political conservatism, but although many would be comfortable with that, some orthodox Anglicans will claim that they are anything but conservative in those senses – they see 'orthodoxy' as a radical commitment they can use to critique and if possible overturn many 'conservative' assumptions. Much the same problem attaches to the word 'traditional(ist)'. Orthodox Anglicans often value the Church's traditions highly and want to see them maintained, but this does not necessarily mean that they are wedded to the 1662 *Book of Common Prayer*, or that they think that bishops should wear mock versions of late Roman aristocratic dress!

As for 'evangelical' and 'catholic', many orthodox Anglicans are happy to embrace either (or both) of these designations, but they have come to represent particular kinds of churchmanship that may reflect orthodoxy without being coterminous with it. The cultural and liturgical associations that these words have acquired mean that we are now faced with people who describe themselves as 'inclusive evangelicals' or 'affirming catholics', using the familiar terms to denote their churchmanship, but qualifying them in ways that are not doctrinally orthodox. In one sense, all evangelicals are 'inclusive' because anybody can become one, and all catholics are 'affirming' of the Church's traditional teachings. But those who describe themselves like this distinguish their positions from standard evangelicalism and catholicism by using the words 'inclusive' and 'affirming' to mean that they accept the so-called 'progressive' or 'revisionist' agenda of the liberals in the Church, with the result that more conventional evangelicals and catholics often disown them. As for 'mainstream', although this word is claimed by an orthodox grouping, it is not clear how mainstream they really are. Do they represent the middle way of classical Anglicanism, or have they adopted a label that they think describes them, even if it is hard to justify in the contemporary climate of opinion?

By calling themselves 'orthodox', doctrinally conservative Anglicans are trying to avoid these potential pitfalls. 'Orthodoxy' can be evangelical and/or catholic, as well as traditional(ist) or mainstream, but it seeks both to embrace these terms and to transcend them. Some may associate the word with the Eastern Orthodox churches, but that is a misunderstanding. It is not that those churches are not orthodox in their own way, but they are culturally distant from most Anglicans and have no formal involvement in internal Anglican affairs. Orthodox Anglicans are not eccentric high church malcontents who will be heading to Constantinople – or still less, to Moscow – any time soon! But unlike the word 'catholic', which now tends to refer to the Roman Catholic Church, the word 'orthodox' is still widely used in contexts that have little or nothing to do with any religious body.[1] It is possible, for example, to be an orthodox communist or an orthodox economist, in which case it means simply a person who is regarded as being faithful to the principles of his/her particular movement or discipline. It is in this way that orthodox Anglicans see themselves – they are claiming to be faithful to the basic tenets of historical Christianity in its Anglican form, even if they manifest that faithfulness in different ways.

The word 'orthodox' does not appear in the Bible, but the concept is fundamental to the New Testament. One

---

[1] It is true that the word 'catholic' can also be used in non-religious senses (like 'a person of catholic tastes', for example) but this is not common in everyday discourse.

of the clearest passages that describes it is 2 Timothy 1:13–14, where Paul tells his disciple Timothy:

> Follow the pattern of the sound words that you have heard from me, in the faith and love that are in Christ Jesus. By the Holy Spirit who dwells within us, guard the good deposit entrusted to you.

Orthodoxy is a 'pattern of sound words' and we as Christians are called to 'guard the good deposit' entrusted to us. We cannot pick and choose what we like about Christianity or reinterpret it to suit particular circumstances. Some 'inclusive evangelicals' and 'affirming catholics' like to describe themselves as 'generously orthodox', but that is a contradiction in terms. To be 'generous' with our orthodoxy by modifying or adapting its fundamental principles to accommodate people or ideas that do not conform to the teaching of the Bible (the only source of the teaching of Jesus that we have) is to lose it altogether. Orthodoxy comes as a package which, in the words of the Athanasian Creed, must be kept 'whole and undefiled' and not be tampered with, diluted or modified in any significant way.[2]

This may seem unloving to some, but it goes back to the teaching of Jesus himself. When he began his ministry, there were people who were attracted to him

---

[2] Orthodoxy can, and sometimes has been, expressed in different ways, often by people who have been influenced by particular philosophical, cultural or historical factors that have not been well understood by others. One of the great benefits of the modern ecumenical movement is that it has rediscovered this and done much to increase the understanding of different orthodox groups that have become estranged over time.

and who wanted to become his followers, but they had reservations, some of which were very understandable. One man wanted leave to bury his father first – surely not an unreasonable request! What did Jesus say to him? 'Leave the dead to bury their own dead. But as for you, go and proclaim the kingdom of God.' To a man who wanted to say goodbye to his family and friends at home before joining the disciples, Jesus replied: 'No one who puts his hand to the plough and looks back is fit for the kingdom of God.'[3] Not much flexibility or generosity there! When confronted by the woman at the well of Samaria, who wanted to argue the case for accepting Samaritan worship as valid, Jesus was direct and to the point: 'You worship what you do not know; we worship what we know, for salvation is from the Jews.'[4] It is true that he then went on to say that the dispute would soon be redundant, because the true worshippers would be called to worship God in spirit and in truth, not in any particular place. But although Samaritans would be welcome to join the Church, their traditions could not be accepted as forerunners of the gospel in the way that those of the Jews were. Hardly the most 'generous' of approaches!

On another occasion, when Jesus shamed a group of men who wanted to stone a woman caught in adultery, he did not excuse the woman's conduct. He refused to condemn her, but he did not condone her behaviour either. Instead, he told her straight: 'Go, and from now on sin no more.'[5] She could certainly be forgiven, but she was still expected to change her way of life. What if she had resorted to prostitution in order to make a living? What if she had claimed to have come from a broken

---

[3] Luke 9:59–62. See also Matthew 8:21–22.

[4] John 4:22.

[5] John 8:11.

home and that she had been socially disadvantaged all her life? The text does not mention anything like that, but it would not have mattered – for followers of Jesus, sin is sin and must not be indulged in, no matter what excuses might be offered in mitigation. Letting her go and giving her the opportunity to sort herself out was about as generous as Jesus ever got. The good deposit of faith cannot abide compromise.

For some people, 'orthodoxy' has a dry academic or intellectual feel, being understood more as a set of doctrines than as a living spirituality, and it must be admitted that the word has sometimes been used in that unhelpful way. Because of this, an orthodox person may be perceived as someone who subscribes to a particular confession of faith and who argues for it in technical theological language that most people find hard to grasp and that often puts them off. What they want is something that will touch the heart and warm the soul, and what they fear is that an exaggerated emphasis on 'orthodoxy' will only quench the Spirit. This is a misapprehension, but it is sufficiently widespread that it requires refutation, not by adopting an academic method of debate, but by offering an alternative approach that will attract those whose hearts are in the right place, but whose minds have not yet been able to grasp the fulness of meaning that the word 'orthodox' conveys.

That orthodoxy is more than a creed or confession of faith set out in quasi-legal language is best illustrated by appealing to the rich tradition of hymnody to which our Church is heir. Anyone can write a hymn, of course, and some odd ones have appeared from time to time, but those that have survived are almost always firmly orthodox, a fact to which they owe their continued popularity. To illustrate the importance of this and its ongoing relevance for us today, let us take a close look at the well-known hymn *The Church's One Foundation*. It is still widely sung in our congregations and was written at another time of crisis, one that has now been largely forgotten. In the 1860s the Anglican world was rocked by the claims of Bishop John Colenso (1814–1883) of Natal (South Africa) that the Bible, and in particular large parts of the Old Testament, was untrue. Colenso had come to that conclusion in his efforts to translate the text into Zulu. His target audience asked him questions about it that he was unable to answer, and so he turned to what was then the still emerging school of liberal German criticism, which was largely dismissive of the Bible's claims to be divine revelation. When word of this reached England, Colenso was censured, but liberal opinion felt that he was being unjustly persecuted and sympathy for his position gradually spread, as did the theology that lay behind it.

Faced with this situation, Samuel John Stone (1839–1900), curate of New Windsor from 1862 to 1870, sat down to write a series of hymns, based on the Apostles' Creed, which he recommended for use by his congregation in order to instil in them the fundamental principles of orthodoxy. The collection of twelve hymns was published as *Lyra Fidelium*, but the only one that became widely known and is still sung today is the one that he wrote to illustrate the 'communion of saints'. Perhaps it owes its survival to the fact that it is a kind of mini-creed in itself, and gives us a practical guide to understanding orthodoxy in terms that can be easily absorbed by non-theologians.

2. Jesus Christ

The Church's one foundation is Jesus
Christ her Lord

She is his new creation by water and
the Word.

From heaven he came and sought her
to be his holy bride

With his own blood he bought her and
for her life he died.

Christianity is Jesus Christ and him crucified. That
is what Paul told the Corinthian church, and it is as
fundamental today as it was then.[1] Everything else that
we say and do is focused around that essential truth. As
Paul went on to add: 'No one can lay a foundation other
than that which is laid, which is Jesus Christ.'[2] Plenty
of people will try to build on that foundation, but what
they construct will be tested and if the construction is
not sound it will be destroyed. What we call 'orthodoxy'
is the building that has stood the test of time, because
it conforms to the parameters of its foundation. This is
why it cannot be dismantled or sectioned off to please
one group or another. The building stands or falls as a
whole, and the witness of the creeds and confessions
that we have inherited reminds us of this.

These statements are important but they are not
the whole story, by any means. They are a structural
framework on and around which the house of God has
been erected. Those who enter the house may not be
aware of how it has been built, but when the storms

---

[1] 1 Corinthians 2:2.
[2] 1 Corinthians 3:11.

come up and the ground starts to shift, the fact that the house is unmoved reveals the solid principles that undergird it.[3] The ancient creeds are a surviving sample of a much larger number of similar texts that were composed in order to ensure that candidates for baptism and for ordained ministry were properly instructed in the basics of the faith, and their emphasis reflects things that were disputed at the time. There was no attempt to be comprehensive, which is one reason why the creeds underwent a process of development as new items were added to them. It was not until the eighth century that the three that we now recognise were stabilised in their present form and inserted into the liturgies of the Church as public declarations of orthodoxy.

Some modern 'revisionists' argue that because these creeds say nothing about lifelong heterosexual monogamy, it cannot be regarded as an integral part of orthodox teaching, but this is a misunderstanding. Nothing was said about it in ancient times, or during the sixteenth century Reformation either, because it was not a matter in dispute. Everybody agreed with it, and there is not a single official document from any church that allows for anything else. On the contrary, services of Holy Matrimony, like the one in the *Book of Common Prayer*, assume lifelong heterosexual marriage without question, as even the 'revisionists' have to acknowledge. Nor does the liturgy shrink from expressing the link between matrimony on the one hand and both the life of the Church and the teaching of the Bible on the other. Before the ceremony begins, the priest points out that it signifies 'unto us the mystical union that is betwixt Christ and his Church',

---

[3] See Matthew 7:24–25.

and then, in addressing the congregation he reminds them: 'Be ye well assured, that so many as are coupled together otherwise than God's Word doth allow are not joined together by God, nor is their matrimony lawful.' It would be easier for the Church to permit polygamy, which is tolerated (though not encouraged) in the Old Testament, than it would be to bless same-sex marriage, which is nowhere even mentioned, let alone permitted. But as far as anyone can tell, no 'revisionist' advocates that! Lifelong heterosexual monogamy is the teaching of the Bible and therefore also the orthodox doctrine of the Church – anything else must be rejected as being contrary to the law of God.

The Church of Jesus Christ is a new creation, brought into being by the one who is the Creator of all things. It does not contradict the first creation but fulfils its purpose, which has been obscured by the rebellion of the fallen angels and by the sin of our first parents. The New Testament's vision is not of something totally new but of something that has been transformed from a material to a spiritual reality. The seed must die, Paul tells the Corinthians, so that the spiritual body can come back from the dead – this is not destruction, but resurrection, which is the very heart of the Christian message.[4] It follows from this that what we do with the seeds of our physical bodies will bear fruit in the spiritual bodies that will rise again from the dead. Or to put it another way, how we think and act in this life is a preparation for the life we shall enjoy in heaven.

In waiting for this transformation to happen, we are responsible for keeping our physical bodies – flesh, mind and soul – as pure and spotless as is possible in a sinful world. The New Testament epistles are full of

---

[4] 1 Corinthians 15:35–58.

injunctions to this effect. Perfection is impossible to achieve, because we live in a society that is in rebellion against God and we have no way of escaping it.[5] But if we cannot change the world around us, we must do all that we can to keep both ourselves and the Church free from the taint of association with people whose behaviour does not correspond to the character of God. As Paul wrote to the Corinthians:

> I am writing to you not to associate with anyone who bears the name of brother if he is guilty of sexual immorality or greed, or is an idolater, reviler, drunkard, or swindler – not even to eat with such a one... Purge the evil person from among you.[6]

The new creation is formed 'by water and the Word'. These two things go together. In Genesis 1 the Word of God went forth to divide the waters, and the creation came into being. In the new creation, the baptismal water bears witness to the promise of the Word, that all who repent and believe will be saved. There are some who claim that water baptism takes effect automatically, as if it were a kind of vaccine that works on the patient whether that patient is aware of it or not. That is not the biblical picture. Water by itself has no power to do anything – it is always (and only) the servant of the Word, a visible illustration of what Christ has come to do. As Jesus said to Nicodemus: 'unless one is born of water and the Spirit, he cannot enter the kingdom of God. That which is born of the flesh is flesh, and that

---

[5] 1 Corinthians 5:9.
[6] 1 Corinthians 5:11, 13.

which is born of the Spirit is spirit. Do not marvel that I said to you, "You must be born again."'[7]

Water baptism teaches us that being born again entails a cleansing and refreshing of our entire being, but only the Holy Spirit, working by the Word of God, can make that a reality. We know only too well that there are thousands of people who have been baptised in water but who have not received the Spirit of God – think of Adolf Hitler and Josef Stalin, to go no further! They were both baptised – Stalin even went to seminary – but would anybody say that they were born again? Large numbers of people today have been baptised, usually in infancy, but it means nothing to them or to anyone else, and some are even resentful of what they received without their knowledge or consent.[8] There are many possible explanations for this, and we cannot judge individual cases. But we can say with complete certainty that water baptism is not a passport to heaven – to be born again is to receive the Spirit of God, and the Spirit comes as the agent of the Word who sends him. In other words, the 'pattern of sound words' is an essential part of the package – without an orthodox profession of faith there can be no guarantee of salvation.

Jesus Christ came from heaven to look for his bride, the Church. In a day and age when the effects of feminism are felt in every walk of life, and when even the pronouns that we use are subject to censure if they do not accommodate it, it is surprising how few people seem to realise that the biblical picture of the Church

---

[7] John 3:5–7.
[8] In France there are reports that some atheists have asked the Roman Catholic Church to erase their names from its baptismal registers, because they deny that they have ever been dedicated to Christ.

is that of a bride adorned for her husband. It is not the only image used to describe the Church, but it is remarkable how closely it is tied to many of the other images. We are called the body of Christ, but since the bride and the bridegroom are joined as one flesh, union with Christ is union with his body. Our bodies are described as the temple of the Spirit, but the body of Christ is also pictured as a temple – Jesus told the Jews that if that temple were to be destroyed, he would raise it up again in three days, as indeed he did![9]

Who was the bride that the Son of God came to find? The Church is portrayed as female, different from him in one way but complementary in another. The idea that God's people are female in relation to him goes back to the Old Testament, and in particular to the witness of the prophets, but it is not a pretty picture. The bride whom Jesus came to find was a harlot, a whore and an adulteress. Hosea was even told to marry such a woman to illustrate just how bad God's chosen people actually were.[10] But whereas Hosea did not enter into his wife's life experience, as we might put it today, Jesus did. As Paul said to the Corinthians: 'For our sake he [God the Father] made him to be sin who knew no sin, so that in him we might become the righteousness of God.'[11]

Our bridegroom became sin for us, but that was not the end of the story. God the Father could not allow his Holy One to see corruption, which is alien to his nature.[12] If he became sin for us, it could only be in order to die and remove the guilt of that sin from us. This is a spiritual experience. We do not cease to be sinners when we are

---

[9] See 1 Corinthians 12:27; Genesis 2:24; John 2:19.
[10] Hosea 1:2.
[11] 2 Corinthians 5:21.
[12] Psalm 16:10; Acts 2:27.

united with Christ, and the fact that we are no longer condemned for what we are by nature is entirely due to his act on our behalf. This is why there can never be any question of salvation by our own efforts (or 'works' as theological tradition has expressed it.) Any attempt on our part to help God out, or to meet him halfway, is doomed to failure, because there is nothing in us that is capable of drawing closer to him. Religions and philosophies of all kinds offer sacrifices, exercises and meditations as ways of getting closer to God, but none of these is of any use, because we cannot contribute anything to our own salvation. The words of Augustus Toplady (1740–1778) in his famous hymn *Rock of Ages* sum up the approach we are called to take:

> Nothing in my hand I bring
> Simply to thy cross I cling
> Naked, come to thee for dress
> Helpless, look to thee for grace
> Foul, I to the fountain fly
> Wash me Saviour, or I die!

This does not mean that sacrifices, exercises and meditations have no place in the Christian life – they most certainly do! But their place is not to earn salvation; it is to demonstrate that we have received it already. We are called to present our bodies as a living sacrifice, not as one that has been killed as an act of propitiation, but as a thanksgiving for the salvation that we have received.[13]

The only way that Christ could make his bride fit for his kingdom was by dying for her – by his blood he paid the price for her sins and by his death he gave her eternal

---

[13] Romans 12:1.

life. This is the heart of the gospel. Theologians call this 'penal substitutionary atonement' because it reconciles us to God (atonement) by the fact that Christ has paid the penalty for our sin that God's justice demands (that's the 'penal' bit) and has taken our place on the cross – substituted himself for us, in other words – and done for us what we cannot do for ourselves. Most Christians do not talk this kind of theological language, but they express the same thing in simple terms of their own: 'Jesus died for me', or as our chosen hymn puts it: 'with his own blood he bought [us] and for [our] life he died.'

This is the heart of the Christian faith, the core of orthodoxy. Every time we come to the Lord's Table and receive the bread and wine that represent his broken body and poured out blood, we bear witness to this truth that has created our identity and that gives us our spiritual life. As material substances, bread and wine can do nothing by themselves. It is all too possible to receive them without discerning the Lord's body, and Paul makes no bones about it – those who do that eat and drink to their own damnation.[14] This is why preparation for the sacrament is so necessary – a preparation that is well provided for in the 1662 *Book of Common Prayer* but that is generally neglected in the modern Church. Is it any wonder that as a Church we are so weak and ill, and that some in our midst have died? What Paul saw in his day, we see in ours – to neglect the orthodox pathway is to court disaster now, just as much as it was then.

---

[14] 1 Corinthians 11:27–32.

3. The Body of the Saved

> Elect from every nation, yet one o'er all
> the earth
> Her charter of salvation, one Lord, one
> faith, one birth
> One holy name she blesses, partakes
> one holy food
> And to one hope she presses, with
> every grace endued.

One of the most important differences between the Old Testament and the New is that in the former, God's people were physically descended from Abraham, Isaac and Jacob. Not all of Abraham's children were Israelites, and there were a few converts from other nations – like Ruth the Moabitess, for example – but they were exceptions. It is fair to say that the Jews of Jesus' day were an ethnic as well as a religious body, as they still are. Christianity changed all that, though not without some difficulty. Jewish Christians tended to believe that the Messiah had come to them, and that anyone who wanted to become a Christian should become a Jew first. Paul, who was archetypically Jewish himself, rejected that and insisted that non-Jews (Gentiles) could become members of the Church without being subjected to the law of Moses, which had been abrogated by the coming of Christ. Feelings on the matter could run high – so high in fact, that Paul had to rebuke Peter, the chief disciple of Jesus himself, for his reluctance to accept the complete equality of Jews and Gentiles in the Church.[1]

---

[1] Galatians 2:11–14.

Before long, however, this problem was resolved and the Church expanded across the Roman world and beyond. The contact language was mainly Greek, but from the beginning, people heard in their own languages the wonderful story of salvation in Christ.[2] Later on, the gospel spread across Western Europe, whose many nationalities were united in a single Church, based in Rome and using Latin as its common tongue. The Protestant Reformation, which insisted on translating the Bible and the liturgy into the vernacular, brought that era to an end, but the principle that every tribe and nation had equal standing before God was at least theoretically preserved. Catholic missionaries, in particular, spread the gospel across Latin America, Africa and Asia. Protestants were slower about this, but after 1800 they picked up momentum, so that today the Bible is available in almost all the major languages of the world and there are churches in virtually every country on the planet. These churches have their own customs and styles of worship, but in terms of belief they are united. There is not one gospel for white people and another for black or Asian ones. No ethnic group holds a special place in the kingdom of God, with the partial – and sometimes controversial – exception of the Jews, a status that derives from the New Testament assertion that the promises made to the Old Testament people of God have not been revoked.[3]

Yet in spite of this, churches in the Western world have been plagued by divisions based not on doctrine but on race and ethnicity. This sad situation is particularly obvious in the United States, where whole denominations are classified as 'black', leaving many

---

[2] Acts 2:8–11.
[3] Romans 11:25–32.

others as 'white' by default, but it is also present in the United Kingdom, where thriving black churches can be found among immigrant communities and most white churches appear to be almost completely ignorant of them. There is no open segregation or discrimination, of course, but divisions of this kind have nevertheless appeared and there is no sign that they are likely to go away anytime soon.

What is even more disturbing though is that within the established, mainly 'white' churches of the Global North, there is a tendency to treat our sisters in the Global South with a certain disdain. This is especially evident in the Anglican Communion, where small churches in the USA, Canada, New Zealand, Scotland and Wales have become bastions of 'progressive' ideas. Unfortunately, although they are in precipitous, and possibly terminal decline, they wield disproportionate influence in the Anglican Communion, most of whose member churches are overwhelmingly orthodox. Australia is a mixed bag, with some strongly orthodox dioceses holding the line against the 'progressive' tide, and Brazil is an anomaly, being a small but highly 'revisionist' province in the Global South. The Church of England is split, with a 'revisionist' faction dominating the upper echelons of the hierarchy, but with a growing body of orthodox opinion lower down the scale, that is no longer as content as it once was to let their opponents dictate Church policy.

Numbers are hard to estimate and often of dubious value, but it is thought that at least 85% of the world's Anglicans belong to orthodox churches, whether they realise it or not. To them may be added a number of loyal Anglicans in 'revisionist' countries that are either keeping their heads down or else have split off to form orthodox denominations of their own. Once again, England is split. There are large and vocal orthodox congregations that are speaking up within the Church, but there are also small splinter groups that have hived off into 'Anglican' denominations that are outside the official structures of the Anglican Communion. What is truly shocking about this is the contempt in which the 85% are held by the 'revisionist' minority. The 'progressives' have introduced new practices, of which same-sex marriage is the most controversial, without consulting the rest of the Anglican world and in defiance of their protests. They seem to believe that they have the right to do this and do not care what anybody else thinks. Not surprisingly, the 85% have felt betrayed by this behaviour, and the result has been the emergence of groups like GAFCON (Global Anglican Futures Conference) and GSFA (Global South Fellowship of Anglicans). They have somewhat different approaches, with GSFA more respectful of traditional Anglican boundaries than GAFCON is, but they overlap and in doctrinal terms they are virtually identical.[4]

In this scenario, the position of the Church of England is unenviable, but disappointing – at least from an orthodox point of view. The English Church authorities have not only refused to dissociate themselves from the 'progressives' but have effectively caved in to their demands. They have cold-shouldered the breakaway Anglican groups in the Western world while at the same time ignoring pleas from the 85% elsewhere. Time and again, bishops and archbishops from the Global South have pleaded with the Archbishop of Canterbury and with the General Synod of the Church

[4] For example, GSFA will not plant churches in Anglican dioceses or provinces that do not belong to it, whereas GAFCON will.

of England not to proceed down the revisionist path, but they have been ignored. The result is that the Anglican Communion is in serious danger of breaking up, especially since neither GAFCON nor GSFA is now prepared to accept the Archbishop of Canterbury as the Communion's titular head. It is a disaster that is almost entirely due to the arrogance of Global North clerics who believe that they have the right to adopt positions which, if they cannot impose them on other Anglicans, they can at least expect those Anglicans to acquiesce in. The idea that as a small minority, they ought to give way and accept that they could be wrong does not seem to occur to them.

This situation makes a mockery of the supposed unity of the Church across the world, and often causes real pain and distress. Many leaders of the 85% have a deep respect for the Church of England (in particular) and some continue to depend on Global North generosity for their institutional viability. In other places there is a very real danger that local churches may be burnt down and local people killed (by Muslim extremists, for example) because of the perceived apostasy of Anglicans who live half a world away from them and who pay no attention to what is going on outside their own neighbourhoods.

Orthodox Anglicans cannot accept this. Those living in England, or elsewhere in the Global North, see themselves as part of the 85% even if they are a minority in their home countries. They may be reluctant to excommunicate 'revisionists' but there is no doubt where their spiritual allegiances lie. They believe in the unity of the worldwide Church and if push comes to shove, they will side with it and not with the so-called 'progressives' nearer to home.

If we look more specifically at the Church of England, where the theological battle is at its most intense, the orthodox are clear about where they stand. Despite the many differences of churchmanship and temperament that divide them, when it comes to the foundations they have no doubts. There is only one charter of salvation, signed in the blood of Jesus Christ, that applies to everybody. There are no special provisions for particular interest groups and there is no discrimination against (or in favour of) people who want the doctrine and practice of the Church to change in order to accommodate them. We know that evangelicals do not feel at home in Anglo-Catholic parishes, nor will traditionalists happily accept women in roles which they believe should be reserved for men, even if the women concerned are excellent and the men are not! But as long as these differences – which can be deeply felt – do not touch on fundamental points of doctrine, the orthodox will come together. It is not easy, but they will make the effort in the interests of a deeper unity that must be preserved at all costs.

What is this deeper unity based on? The first and most fundamental point of agreement is that there is one holy Name that we worship. This is the God of the Bible, the Holy Trinity of Father, Son and Holy Spirit. Who they are and how they act in our salvation is clearly set out in the classical creeds, traditionally (if erroneously) attributed to the apostles, the first Council of Nicaea and St Athanasius, the great defender of Nicene orthodoxy in the fourth century.[5] Almost all Christians

---

[5] In reality, the Apostles' Creed as we know it reached its present form in the eighth century, though it is based on earlier texts going back at least 600 years before that. The Nicene Creed is most probably the product of the first Council of Constantinople in AD 381, which sought to

everywhere – not just Anglicans – subscribe to the substance of these three Creeds, even if there are ongoing debates about some things, like the procession of the Holy Spirit, depending on the theological model adopted for explaining inner-Trinitarian relations.[6] There are also some residual differences in the Eastern Churches over the Christology of the Council of Chalcedon, which is affirmed in the Athanasian Creed, but it is now generally agreed that the difficulty lies in finding the best way to express a theology that in substance all sides hold in common. If that is so, it is a timely reminder that the Creeds, important as they are, are nevertheless incomplete expressions of an underlying orthodoxy that believers intuit from their shared experience of the divine Trinity, which like all personal relationships, defies detailed human description.

The next thing is that as orthodox believers, we share one holy food – the bread and wine of communion with the risen, ascended and glorified Lord. There have been endless arguments over this both within the Anglican tradition and in the wider Christian world. Should

reaffirm the faith of the first Council of Nicaea (AD 325), but did not originate there. The so-called Athanasian Creed, also known as the *Quicunque vult*, from its first two words, probably comes from late fifth-century Gaul (now France), but was attached to Athanasius (AD 296–373) because he was acknowledged as the great, and often only, defender of Nicene orthodoxy.

[6] This is an extremely complicated question, usually referred to as the *Filioque* controversy, so called from the Latin for 'and the Son', which was added to the Nicene Creed in Spain sometime in the late sixth century, probably in order to affirm the complete equality of the divinity of the Father and the Son, which was denied by the so-called Arians.

we use leavened or unleavened bread? Fermented wine or unfermented grape juice? What, if anything, happens to the elements once they are consecrated? Who is entitled to preside at the Lord's Table and/or to participate in the communion itself? If we stand back and try to look at these things objectively, we shall soon see that some of the debates are rooted in philosophical differences about the relationship between matter and spirit, while others are basically housekeeping issues that do not affect the main point. Wherever we land on the spectrum of these debates though, the fundamental principle remains the same. It is well expressed in the famous hymn of the Scottish divine Horatius Bonar (1808–1889):

> Here O my Lord I see thee face to face
> Here would I touch and handle
> things unseen
> Here would I grasp with firmer hand
> thy grace
> And all my weariness upon thee lean.

On this, all orthodox believers are agreed and the theological barriers to Table fellowship, while they do not disappear, nevertheless fade into the background as we come face to face with the presence of the Lord who is the Spirit.[7]

Finally, orthodox believers share the same eschatological vision. We have one hope to which we are headed, the final consummation of all things in the kingdom of God. We live in a world where technological progress

---

[7] It should be noted that Anglicans invite all baptised members in good standing of whatever church they belong to, to share with us in Holy Communion. Unfortunately, that openness is not always reciprocated by other churches.

exists alongside existential despair. At one level, life has never been easier for most people than it is today. Poverty and disease are still with us, to be sure, but scientific developments suggest that these material ills will eventually be overcome. Yet at the same time, never have there been more unhappy people, surrounded by affluence yet unable to find contentment. For many, wealth and physical independence have created a world of loneliness, in which old people are left to die unnoticed and unmourned, relationships come under unbearable strain and fall apart, and nobody feels safe anymore. Orthodox Christians see this all around them, but they do not share in the general spirit of despair. Like the dying Henry Francis Lyte (1793–1847), they sing in their hearts:

> Hold thou thy cross before my
> dying eyes
> Shine through the gloom and point
> me to the skies
> Heaven's morning breaks and earth's
> vain shadows flee
> In life, in death, O Lord, abide
> with me!

Like John Bunyan's pilgrim Christian, the orthodox see the vision of the heavenly city waiting to receive them and hear the trumpets sounding on the other side. Christians are people of hope, who await the coming of the Lord in glory. Even our celebration of his death in the Eucharist is done in hope. As the apostle Paul told the Corinthians: 'As often as you eat this bread and drink the cup, you proclaim the Lord's death until he comes.'[8] Or in the words of the Nicene Creed: 'He shall

---

[8] 1 Corinthians 11:26.

come again with glory to judge both the living and the dead; whose kingdom shall have no end.' When that will be we have no idea and it is pointless to speculate. But come he will, and then the hearts of all people will be opened and the just judgement of God will be given. For those who have been faithful all along, it scarcely matters whether we shall be dead or alive at his coming, because either way we shall rise to live and reign with him in eternity. This is the hope that is in us, and the light that guides us along the pilgrim way to the heavenly city.

4. Despised by the World

Though with a scornful wonder men
see her sore oppressed

By schisms rent asunder, by
heresies distressed

Yet saints their watch are keeping,
their cry goes up 'How long?'

And soon the night of weeping shall
be the morn of song.

The prologue to John's Gospel is justly famous as a statement of God's plan and purpose in sending his Son into the world, but it contains one jarring line: 'He came to his own, and his own people did not receive him.'[1] Later on Jesus assures his disciples that God will not be slow to avenge his people when the time comes, but he too adds a note of caution:

> Will not God give justice to his elect, who cry to him day and night? Will he delay long over them? I tell you, he will give justice to them speedily. Nevertheless, when the Son of Man comes, will he find faith on earth?[2]

Christians are agreed that the gospel is the 'greatest story ever told'. How can it be that a humble carpenter from a small nation could change the world by his life, death and resurrection? How is it possible that the hope of ages, sought by the greatest philosophers and thinkers of all time but not found by any of them,

---

[1] John 1:11.
[2] Luke 18:7–8.

should have come to a group of uneducated peasants, who were empowered by the Spirit of God to proclaim the good news to the ends of the earth, yet who went to their deaths, many of them, persecuted by the very people they wanted to see saved? There is a mystery here that is almost impossible to fathom. It begins with the Jewish people, chosen by God but tortured from one generation to the next by foes both within and without. No sooner had God revealed himself to Jacob and given him the name Israel, than his people went down to Egypt, where they were enslaved for hundreds of years before making their miraculous escape. But the newly freed Israelites were soon mired in idolatry, lost in the desert and unable to coalesce as a nation. After a brief respite under the great kings David and his son Solomon they were divided and spent their strength fighting their neighbours and each other for several centuries, until they were finally carted off into exile.

They were eventually able to return to the land that God had promised them, but they did not regain their sovereignty. After a brief period of independence from about 165 to 63 BC, they came under Roman rule, from which they never escaped. Rebellion led to the destruction of Jerusalem, and for nearly 2,000 years they were condemned to wander the earth – despised and often persecuted by people who in theory worshipped the same God. Finally, after a concerted attempt to wipe them out, they were able to re-establish a state in their ancient homeland of Palestine, only to discover that the inhabitants of that land did not welcome them. Ever since 1948 they have been under siege from their neighbours, who are determined to drive them back into the sea from which they came. They may not succeed in the short term, but the state of Israel cannot sleep soundly. Sooner or later, somehow or other, it will be fighting for its life, and if God does not intervene to save it, nobody else will.

Christians are often uneasy when they reflect on this history, not least because many of the persecutors of the Jews were acting in the name of Christ, however hypocritical and insincere they may have been. But the amazing fact is that, in spite of everything, Israel is still with us. The Assyrians, Babylonians, ancient Greeks and Romans – not to mention the Ammonites, Moabites, Edomites, Canaanites, Philistines and the rest – have all disappeared, but the Jews have survived and have even resurrected their ancient language on the soil that God promised to Abraham 4,000 years ago. There has never been anything like it in human history, and yet what other nation has suffered to the extent that they have? As Hebrews 11:35–38 reminds us:

> Some were tortured, refusing to accept release, so that they might rise again to a better life. Others suffered mocking and flogging, and even chains and imprisonment. They were stoned, they were sawn in two, they were killed with the sword. They went about in skins of sheep and goats, destitute, afflicted mistreated – of whom the world was not worthy – wandering about in deserts and mountains, and in dens and caves of the earth.

Such is the story of the faithful men and women of Israel. But what about us Christians? Jesus said: 'Blessed are you when others revile you and persecute you and utter all kinds of evil against you falsely on my account. Rejoice and be glad, for your reward is great in heaven, for so persecuted they the prophets who were before you.'[3] Paul added: 'All who desire to live a godly life in Christ Jesus will be persecuted, while evil people and imposters will go on from bad to worse, deceiving and being deceived.'[4] We cannot say that we have not been warned!

When we look at the historical record, we can see that for the first three hundred years of its existence, the Church did indeed suffer persecution from the outside world. The message of salvation was not well received, either by those to whom it was first given (the Jews) or by those to whom it was subsequently preached (the Gentiles). Martyrdom became a badge of sanctity, a guarantee that the martyr would go straight to heaven after death for the name of Christ. Yet from the very beginning, the greatest danger to the Church came from within – from schismatics and heretics who worked to destroy its unity and corrupt its teaching. No sooner had Paul preached the gospel to the Galatians than false apostles appeared, to contradict his message and lead people back into the spiritual bondage from which he had liberated them.[5] The Corinthian church was riven by internal disputes that even visits from the apostle or his deputies were unable to resolve. Indeed, most of the epistles that we now have in the New Testament were written for this very reason, and anyone naive enough to think that everything would be fine if we could only go back to the early years of the Church and relive the good old days has failed to read them properly. There was never a golden age of Christianity from which we have fallen away – what was true in Paul's day has been true, one way or another, ever since.

---

[3] Matthew 5:11–12.

[4] 2 Timothy 3:12.

[5] See Galatians 1:6–7.

Orthodox believers are well aware of this. Persecution of the traditional kind still exists, and as Rupert Shortt has demonstrated, Christians around the world now suffer from religious discrimination more than the members of any other faith group.[6] But in Western countries, opportunities for martyrdom are thankfully rare and the Church has never suffered to the extent that the Jews have. We are blessed in that respect, but a case can be made for saying that the peace that we have known may have contributed to a weakening of our commitment to Christ rather than served as a platform for greater zeal in reaching out to the unsaved world. That is an argument for another time, but what is certain is that the Church today is as riven by schism and heresy as it has ever been, and that some of the greatest offenders in this respect have held high positions in it and acted more or less with impunity. For example, on All Saints' Day 2023 no fewer than forty-four bishops of the Church of England (fifteen diocesans and twenty-nine suffragans) issued a letter in which they openly advocated the acceptance of same-sex marriage, even for the clergy.[7] They knew full well that this would inflame an already existing division in their own ranks – they said as much in the letter itself – but that did not deter them. What they were proposing is contrary to the Church's teaching, and therefore arguably heretical, and it is certain to lead to at least informal schism (papered over, perhaps, as 'alternative episcopal oversight') but this did not restrain them. In their view, they have history on their side and are

---

[6] See R. Shortt, *Christianophobia: A Faith Under Attack* (London: Rider, 2012).

[7] Francis Martin, 'Don't delay guidance allowing priests to be in same-sex marriages, say 44 bishops', *Church Times*, 1 November 2023.

determined to advance their cause, however many casualties there may be along the way.

It is obvious from that letter, and from other statements of a similar kind, that the opposition these bishops face comes mainly from the orthodox within the Church, from those who cannot sacrifice the truth for the sake of the superficial harmony that now goes by the name of 'good disagreement'. Between right and wrong there is no such thing as 'good disagreement', because it means tolerating error – and in this case sin – as if it has equal rights with the faith once delivered to the saints. No orthodox person can accept that. None of us has asked to be put in this situation and none desires it. All orthodox people would far rather get on with the job of evangelising a nation that is hard of hearing, and some Anglicans have even been led into schisms of their own, setting up 'pure' congregations outside the established structures because they cannot in conscience submit to what they see as a corrupted authority. Their frustration is understandable, but 'pure' churches do not exist, and trying to create them merely weakens the orthodox witness within the establishment. The ironic result is that the Church is 'sore oppressed' by the very people who claim to be its strongest supporters, whether they are 'revisionist' heretics trying to update our doctrine for a godless age, or hyper-orthodox schismatics who want to turn us into a sect.

In such conditions, the orthodox who remain within the institutional Church hardly know which way to turn. To oppose the 'revisionists' by employing their own tactics of deception and manipulation would be to lose the spiritual battle, even if it succeeded in winning a few votes in some synod or other. To secede from the Church, on the other hand, would be a dereliction of duty that amounted to surrender and defeat without firing a shot. So, what should they do?

Here the orthodox have a weapon that the 'revisionists' do not understand. That weapon is prayer. The saints are keeping watch, unknown to the public and unseen, even in the Church itself. How many unsung heroes of the faith, men and women who are publicly invisible but who draw close to God in the privacy of their hearts, are crying out to him: 'How long?'[8] They see the problem and they engage in the battle with a weapon that their adversaries cannot fathom. For the orthodox, God is not a word thrown around to justify their own programmes and prejudices, but the sovereign Lord of heaven and earth, who can and will thwart the machinations of those opposed to him, and probably in ways that we cannot now foresee or imagine. Like the saints of old, the orthodox of today are 'strangers and exiles on the earth', people who in spiritual terms are resident aliens but who in fact are the secret agents of the Creator and Redeemer of us all.[9]

For some, of course, their prayers will lead to direct action. There are orthodox people in potentially influential positions who have a duty to use what God has given them, regardless of the potential cost. This is the lesson that Mordecai taught to Esther, when she demurred at the thought of interceding with the king of Persia for the salvation of her people: 'Who knows whether you have not come to the kingdom for such a time as this?'[10] It takes great courage to stand up to the forces arrayed against us, but as God said to Eli the priest when his family were abusing their status: 'Those

---

[8] Revelation 6:10.

[9] Hebrews 11:13.

[10] Esther 4:14.

who honour me I will honour.'[11] We may not be burnt at the stake in literal terms. But in the sight of God, our witness to the truth will be just as important as that of Hugh Latimer and Nicholas Ridley, who comforted themselves in their last moments with the assurance that their sacrifice would create a light in England that would never go out.[12] The memory of that day – 16 October 1555 – is etched on the collective conscience of the Church of England and will stay there as long as there are faithful men and women who will continue to keep the candle of truth alight.

The night of struggle against schism and heresy will be long and painful, with much weeping as we endure setbacks and apparent failure. But the promise of God is sure – weeping may tarry for the night, but joy comes with the morning.[13] Our distress is for a time, but our deliverance is at hand if only we watch and pray for it to come.

---

[11] 1 Samuel 2:30.
[12] The actual recorded words of Hugh Latimer are: 'Play the man, Master Ridley, we shall this day light such a candle, by God's grace, in England, as I trust shall never be put out.'
[13] Psalm 30:5.

5. Spiritual Warfare

Mid toil and tribulation and tumult of
her war
She waits the consummation of peace
for evermore
Till with the vision glorious her
longing eyes are blessed
And the great Church victorious shall
be the Church at rest.

There was a time in the history of the Church when the idea of going to war for peace and justice was greatly admired. In 1914, pulpits rang with a call to arms and the message conveyed was that the forces of righteousness had to be marshalled to defeat an ungodly enemy. In the United Kingdom, the rhetoric was understood to mean that plucky Britons had to go to Belgium to fight the wicked Germans, and many rallied to the call. Unfortunately, things were more complicated than that. For a start, the Germans heard the same message, but interpreted it in the opposite way. They were not particularly anti-British – attacking the French and the Russians was much more their style – and they wished that Britain had stayed out of the conflict, but the result was the same. Men were killed, at first in their hundreds, then in their thousands, and finally even in their millions. When it was all over, Europe lay in ruins, disillusionment – not least with the churches and their false gospel – was rampant, and there was no lasting solution to the problems that had caused the war in the first place. Twenty years later it was all re-enacted, with equally devastating consequences, and the world has never really been at peace since.

Christians were caught up in this in their own way, though they tried to put a spiritual gloss on what otherwise appeared as rampant militarism. The historically disastrous Crusades came back into fashion, and the word was recycled to refer to evangelistic rallies that aimed to convert the masses. Hymns like *Onward Christian Soldiers* were frequently sung and interpreted in moral and spiritual, as opposed to military, terms. But as the reality of war was brought home to people – not least through the medium of television, which enabled viewers to experience something of the battlefield in their own homes – the mood changed. Crusading is no longer mentioned as much as it once was, and martial hymns have been all but banned from public worship. Today, the churches ring with messages of peace, harmony and love, even though none of these things is especially evident, either within or without the confines of their sacred spaces. The mood music has changed, and with it a tradition that goes back to the early Church has been set aside. The desert monks who warred with evil spirits are occasionally remembered in some circles, but on the whole they have been forgotten. The spiritual dimension of the knights of King Arthur's round table, who went in search of the Holy Grail, has been quietly ignored.[1] The battle cries of the Reformers and the Puritans have been sidelined, even by those who honour them. Spiritual warfare, in a word, has gone out of fashion.

But as anyone who reads the Bible can attest, spiritual warfare is a constant and enduring feature of the life of God's people. It can be traced back to Abraham and through the history of ancient Israel, where the

[1] The Holy Grail was the cup that Jesus used at the Last Supper. The Arthurian legends are mythical, of course, but they were meant to convey spiritual truths.

prophets were constantly leading the charge against the Gentiles without and the idolaters within the nation. Jesus went into the desert to do battle with the devil, and the apostle Paul did not hesitate to use military images and metaphors to describe the struggles of the Christian life. Here as elsewhere, the orthodox within the Church are out of step with the world around us. For us, spiritual warfare is a daily reality in which we confront the world, the flesh and the devil. Unlike the 'revisionists' in the Church, who want to be part of the world, who glory in the flesh, and who do not believe in the devil, the orthodox see themselves at war with everything that these terms represent. That they often discover that their targets are the so-called 'progressive' members of the Church is disconcerting but hardly surprising. If one's fellow citizens consort with the enemy, even in the interests of 'peacekeeping', it is only to be expected that sooner or later they will be caught in the crossfire.

The key biblical text for spiritual warfare is Ephesians 6:10–20, in which the apostle Paul exhorts us to put on the whole armour of God. Paul starts with first principles and illustrates them as he goes along. The orthodox spiritual warrior is called to be strong – not in his/her own strength, but in the power of the Lord. The fundamental enemy we face is not material but spiritual – it is the devil. Satan usually does not reveal himself directly but comes to us through intermediaries who may appear to be very impressive and even intimidating – they are the rulers and authorities who control this darkness of a world that has fallen away from God. In the Church of England, we occasionally hear that the 'progressive' agenda must be promoted because otherwise members of parliament will start advocating for disestablishment – as clear an example as one could wish for of the situation that Paul is warning us against. Add to that pressures from the press, the audio-visual media and the general tenor of society in which it is not polite to speak about one's religious convictions, and the spiritual forces of evil that the apostle talks about suddenly spring to life.

Here the orthodox have a distinct advantage because they know their enemy. History tells us that armies are often well equipped to fight the last war, and so are unprepared for the difficulties that they are going to face in the next one. The Americans who went into Vietnam had no experience of guerilla warfare in the jungle and were accordingly defeated by a foe that was less well equipped but much better prepared for the realities of the situation. More recently, Israel has gone into Gaza with conventional tanks and other weapons, but has been frustrated by the defences of Hamas, the terrorist organisation that controls the Gaza Strip, which has constructed a maze of tunnels in which the enemy can only be attacked by old-fashioned hand-to-hand combat, and where the integration of the tunnels with residential and other such buildings means that victory can only come at the cost of numerous civilian lives. In the spiritual world, the wiles of the devil are forever finding new ways of tormenting the people of God and we must be constantly aware of them. Of course, our 'revisionist' friends cannot even begin to engage in this battle, since for the most part they do not believe in the devil at all. That he is their commander-in-chief has escaped their notice entirely!

The successful soldier is the one who goes into battle prepared for every eventuality, and it is this that the apostle Paul concentrates on. First of all, he mentions the 'belt of truth'. It is in the belt that the soldier stores his weapons, and the truth is indispensable. We need to recognise that same-sex marriage is a lie, that transgenderism is a fantasy, and that conforming to the ways of the world is a mirage that will disappear as soon as we try to achieve it. The truth is that the world is at enmity with God and if we do not acknowledge that fact, we shall be defeated from the start.

The second requirement, closely tied to the first, is that we should put on the 'breastplate of righteousness'. This is vitally important, especially for orthodox people, because it is sadly possible to profess the truth without living it out. Theory and practice have to coincide, so that the charge of hypocrisy does not stick. We must remember that most people see how we behave and evaluate our doctrine from that – not the other way round. There can be no greater harm done than that caused by theoretically orthodox people who do not live out their convictions, and we must always be on our guard against that.

Next comes the charge to put on the 'shoes' of 'the gospel of peace'. Peace with God is the foundation of everything else that we think, say and do. If we are not in the right relationship with him, not because of unbelief but because of something that is troubling us, then that unease will communicate itself and our witness will be compromised. If we are anxious about something, we may not be trusting the Lord in the way that we should, and as with the absence of righteousness, that will be obvious to onlookers, whether we say anything or not. Orthodox people are not tossed about by every wind of doctrine.[2] We know whom we have believed and are content to trust God for whatever comes next!

---

[2] Ephesians 4:14–15.

Following on from that, come 'the shield of faith', 'the helmet of salvation' and 'the sword of the Spirit'. Without faith we can do nothing. It is our protection in times of trouble, the armour that can 'extinguish all the flaming darts of the evil one.' Those who walk with the Lord, and especially those who are called to minister in his name, know only too well how we are attacked, and we must be prepared to resist. Our heads must be covered with the helmet of salvation – the reminder that the gospel is a message for those who are perishing and that our minds must always be protected by that knowledge. It is easy to think that we know better than God, that we have somehow 'come of age' and no longer need to hear the old, old story of Jesus and his love. We can quickly be led astray by new ideas or sidetracked into things that are good in themselves but that miss the point of Christ's coming into the world. The helmet of salvation is there to remind us how desperately our minds need to be protected against that!

Finally, there is the sword of the Spirit, the only part of our armour that is itself a weapon. The sword of the Spirit is the Word of God – Holy Scripture. This is an important truth that is sometimes obscured by people who want to make a false distinction between the Bible and Christian experience, which is guided and governed by the pattern of the words of Scripture. There may be other things that can happen to us – mystical experiences, for example – but although they may be genuine, it is by the yardstick of Scripture that they must be measured.[3] Any experience that contradicts Scripture, or that claims to go beyond it, is deceptive and must be treated with the utmost caution. It is here that the orthodox are wary of charismatic phenomena

---

[3] Paul addresses this question in 2 Corinthians 12:2–5.

that do not have a solid biblical grounding. We cannot go to the extreme of saying that speaking in tongues (for example) is impossible or that it has ceased in the life of the Church. There is no statement to that effect in the Bible and it is not up to us to rule it out merely because we have not encountered it, or because what we have encountered strikes us as unconvincing. But at the same time, we have to resist claims made by some people that God has spoken to them privately and told them to think, say or do something that is not attested in Scripture and may even be contrary to its teaching.

To pray in the Spirit is to pray with our minds as well as with our emotions. We do not have to adopt a special voice or sound histrionic, but what we say in our prayers must come from the heart. Prayer may be liturgical in form, and Anglicans in particular know how powerful the words of a well-known liturgy can be, but our prayers must never be purely formal. They must spring from the heart. Set texts, of which the Lord's Prayer is the best known, may guide us and help us, but we must always ensure that the words are Spirit-filled and that they lead us into an ever-deeper communion with God.

The end of our warfare is the peace that passes understanding, which only God can give.[4] It is a peace that is illuminated by the glorious vision of the triumph of the saints in eternal light. The book of Revelation has been interpreted in many ways and on many different levels, but this at least is clear – it is the story of spiritual warfare and how it results in the victory of the Lamb of God who was slain from before the foundation of the world.[5] The vision of the New Jerusalem in Revelation 21 is that of the Church descending from heaven as

---

[4] Philippians 4:7.
[5] Revelation 13:8.

Christ's bride. The Spirit and the bride say 'Come'.[6] The Bible ends on that note of triumphal invitation, and the reminder of the supreme importance of orthodoxy in the Christian life:

> I warn everyone who hears the words of the prophecy of this book: if anyone adds to them, God will add to him the plagues described in this book, and if anyone takes away from the words of the book of this prophecy, God will take away his share in the tree of life and in the holy city, which are described in this book.[7]

No additions and no subtractions – the revelation is what it is and must be accepted as a whole. Orthodoxy comes as a complete package, not as a series of options from which we can pick and choose, or which we can 'generously' excuse some people from absorbing and observing. None of us is perfect of course, but as we grow in the Spirit, so we grow in the knowledge of the Word and so our minds are conformed increasingly to the mind of Christ, who alone is the way, the truth and life.[8]

---

[6] Revelation 22:17.
[7] Revelation 22:18–19.
[8] John 14:6.

6. The Communion of Saints

> Yet she on earth hath union with God
> the Three in One
>
> And mystic sweet communion with
> those whose rest is won
>
> O happy ones and holy! Lord, give us
> grace that we
>
> Like them the meek and lowly, on high
> may dwell with thee.

The life of orthodoxy is the life of the communion of saints – those who labour in the Church militant here on earth and those who enjoy the rest of the Church triumphant in heaven. The lynchpin is the union we have with God the Holy Trinity. To describe this in detail would take a whole book, and even then we could do little more than scratch the surface of the mystery. The Trinity is a communion of life in itself. God is a God of love, but to have love we must have a plurality of persons. If there were only a single person in the Godhead there would be no internal relationships in him and love could not exist. There are some people who say that God created the world in order to have something to love, but that cannot be right. Of course, God loves what he has made, but his love must be perfect in his own being and not dependent on something that he has created. This is why there is a plurality of persons in God. The Father loves the Son in perfection and the Son loves the Father with the same perfection with which he is loved. Together, the Father and the Son love the Holy Spirit, who may be described as our 'contact point' with God. By this we mean what Paul says in Galatians 4:6: 'And because you are sons, God has sent the Spirit of his Son into our hearts, crying "Abba, Father".' The Spirit unites us with the Son who pleads for us with the Father on the basis of the sacrifice that he has made to redeem us from our sins. When the Spirit comes into our lives, the Father and the Son come with him, so that we enjoy the fellowship of all three at once.[1]

Orthodox Christians understand this in slightly different ways, and unfortunately these have caused schism in the universal Church. The Eastern Orthodox confess that the Holy Spirit proceeds from the Father, as John 15:26 clearly states, but they interpret this to mean that he proceeds from the Father *alone*, which the text does not say. Protestants and Catholics add that the Spirit is also the Spirit of the Son, as we read in Galatians 4:6. Where there is uncertainty, and therefore disagreement, is in the nature of the relationship between the Spirit and the Son. To the Eastern mind, there is only one source of divinity, and that is the Father. To say that the Spirit proceeds from the Father and the Son is therefore to say that there are two sources of divinity – in effect, creating two gods. The Western (Catholic and Protestant) mind says that the Holy Spirit is also the Spirit of the Son, because if he were not, our relationship with the Son would be different from our relationship with the Father. Needless to say, the Western churches do not believe that there are two sources of divinity in God, nor do the Eastern ones deny that there is a sense in which the Holy Spirit is the Spirit of the Son as well as of the Father. We both affirm the teaching of John 15:26 and of Galatians 4:6, but our different models of the Trinity make it difficult for us to come to a common way of explaining our shared

---

[1] John 14:23.

48

experience. The institutional churches have fallen out over this, but that seldom prevents ordinary believers from enjoying each other's fellowship. We have not yet found a way to express the Trinitarian relations in a way that will accommodate everybody's concerns, but we keep trying, because we know that what we want to confess is the same. Here we see as clearly as anywhere that true orthodoxy goes beyond the limitations of human language, not in a way that contradicts our reason, but in a way that transcends it and proves, as God himself said to Isaiah, that:

> My thoughts are not your thoughts, neither are your ways my ways, declares the Lord. For as the heavens are higher than the earth, so are my ways higher than your ways and my thoughts than your thoughts.[2]

We must leave it there, but where the inner life of the Trinity is concerned, the time will come when what we now see through a glass darkly will be revealed to us face to face. Now we know in part, but then we shall know fully, just as we are fully known.[3]

It is in and through the Holy Trinity that we have 'mystic sweet communion with those whose rest is won.' The Christians who have gone before us are gathered round the throne of God and it is in and through him that we are united with them. A picture of this is given to us in the accounts of the Transfiguration of Jesus that we find in the Gospels.[4] The disciples whom Jesus took up the mountain – Peter, James and John – have a vision

---

[2] Isaiah 55:8–9.
[3] 1 Corinthians 13:12.
[4] Matthew 17:1–9; Mark 9:2–9; Luke 9:28–36.

of Jesus in his heavenly glory, and Jesus appears to be speaking to Moses and Elijah, the archetypes of the Old Testament law and prophets. But notice that Peter, James and John do not speak to Moses and Elijah directly, nor do Moses and Elijah speak to them. All communication – and therefore communion – with them is in and through Jesus. It is important to stress this because there is an exaggerated form of piety that suggests that we can ask the saints in heaven to intercede with God on our behalf. We are indeed one with them, but our communication is through Christ in the Spirit. It makes no sense to speak to a saint in heaven and to ask him or her to pray to Christ on our behalf, when we can only communicate with that saint (to the extent that we can) in and through Christ! Here we are dealing with pious intentions gone wrong, a danger that orthodox people are liable to fall into. We may say something that is right in theory, but we must also ensure that we apply it in a way that is right in practice, and here is a good example of how it is possible to do one but not the other!

Our fellowship is with the Church triumphant in heaven, those who have attained to their rest and are gathered in praise and adoration around the throne of God. They are happy, of course, but they are also holy, and that is a note that sounds throughout the Bible. It is one of the ironies of life that the people we call 'saints' would be the first ones to deny that they are somehow special in the sight of God. As the hymn puts it, they are 'meek and lowly', essential qualifications for true holiness. The apostle Paul sets the example when he writes to the Ephesians: 'To me, though I am the very least of all the saints, this grace was given, to preach to the Gentiles the unsearchable riches of Christ.'[5] Nor

---

[5] Ephesians 3:8.

did he think very highly of the Gentiles to whom he was called to preach:

> Do not be deceived: neither the sexually immoral, nor idolaters, nor adulterers, nor men who practise homosexuality, nor thieves, nor the greedy, nor drunkards, nor revilers, nor swindlers will inherit the kingdom of God. And such were some of you. But you were washed, you were sanctified, you were justified in the name of the Lord Jesus Christ and by the Spirit of our God.[6]

The pedigree of the average 'saint' is nothing to boast about! This is the true spirit of those who are orthodox believers. We do not claim to be superior to others – on the contrary, we are only too well aware of our sins, our weaknesses and our failures. We do not claim the highest places in the congregation on the basis of our achievements, or on the assumption that because we got there first we deserve greater recognition. We are all less than the least of all saints – Paul actually had to invent a word to describe just how lowly he was in the sight of God, and that word applies to us just as much as it applied to him. Orthodox Christians welcome fellow sinners with open arms, because we know what they are like – one way or another, we have been in their shoes ourselves. But we welcome them, not to affirm them as they are, but to offer them the precious gift of the gospel – cleansing from the guilt of sin, sanctification in the Spirit and justification by faith in the name of Christ alone. This is what we have to offer, this is our belief, here is the Rock on which we stand. We can do no other.

---

[6] 1 Corinthians 6:9–11.

7. Why Orthodoxy Matters

A bride must love her husband as he is, and not as she would like him to be. The old joke that a wedding can be summed up as 'aisle, altar, hymn' (I'll alter him) is just that – a joke. Many a bride has tried it, only to discover that it does not work. In human terms she may have a good case, but when the bridegroom is Jesus Christ she has none at all. Yet so many people come to the Saviour wanting him to accommodate their wishes and expecting that he will. Their Jesus is a 'loving' God who affirms them as they are, delivers them from their low self-esteem and generally does whatever they want. This is not the Christ of the Bible! Jesus said: 'You are my friends if you do what I command you.'[1] He told his disciples: 'If anyone would come after me, let him deny himself and take up his cross and follow me. For whoever would save his life will lose it, but whoever loses his life for my sake will find it.'[2] This is the one we are married to – a demanding husband who insists on being obeyed, but also the source and guarantor of our life. We cannot do without him, but we must take him as he is and follow him wherever he leads us.

This is not a simple matter. Jesus said: 'Enter by the narrow gate. For the gate is wide and the way is easy that leads to destruction, and those who enter by it are many. For the gate is narrow and the way is hard that leads to life, and those who find it are few.'[3] Fast forward 2,000 years and the meaning is obvious – the pathway of inclusive evangelicalism, affirming catholicism and

---

[1] John 15:14.
[2] Matthew 16:24–25.
[3] Matthew 7:13–14.

generous orthodoxy is easy, and there are many who prefer it. But the way of truth, the way of self-sacrifice, the way of righteousness – that is hard, and those who take it are few. Orthodoxy is not a majority faith. In every age, true believers are unusual and they can stick out like a sore thumb. They are never popular, and the message they have to bring will be resisted, not because it is false, but because those who hear it know that it is true – and it is for that reason that they do not want it. Yet God does not leave himself without a witness. Even in the case of Sodom and Gomorrah, he would have spared the cities if he had found as few as ten righteous people in them.[4] Sadly, there were none at all, and so the cities were wiped out. Our Western societies have not sunk to that level – at least, not yet. The outlook may be bleak, but the promises of God remain and as long as there are people who cling to them we shall be spared. To those who were anxious about the future, Jesus said: 'Fear not, little flock, for it is your Father's good pleasure to give you the kingdom.'[5] Armed with that assurance we are ready for battle and let us not fool ourselves – there will be a battle indeed, in this and every generation, until Jesus comes again in glory.

Orthodoxy matters because it is the way to life promised by the Saviour to all who follow him in sincerity and truth. We cannot pick and choose what we like about him and discard the rest. We cannot make excuses for people and types of behaviour that God has condemned – the spectre of Sodom and Gomorrah hangs over us still. To follow Jesus is to follow him completely and wholeheartedly – there can be no turning back for those who want to reign with him in the kingdom of heaven.

---

[4] Genesis 18:32.
[5] Luke 12:32.

It is sometimes observed that among the 'revisionists' there are people who have known the way of truth but who have departed from it. This may be explained by saying that young people tend to be dogmatic and idealistic, and that many who become Christians at that time in their lives subsequently grow out of the naive faith that they then accepted.

There may be some truth in that, but it is not the whole story. Jesus' parable of the sower gives us a different perspective on this.[6] The seed is sown on all kinds of ground, but it is received differently. In some cases, it stays on the surface, and is eaten by the birds – these are the people who cannot make head or tail of the gospel and so they reject it. Sometimes it falls on rocky ground, where it is initially received with joy, but the rocks prevent it from putting down roots, and when adversity comes, it withers and dies. In still other cases, the seed falls on thorny ground. At first, it appears to prosper, but then the weeds spring up and choke it. Finally, some of the seed falls on good ground, and there it bears fruit. It is not hard to see that it is this last kind of ground that produces orthodoxy, and the resilience that lasts. Those of us who produce this good fruit can only look at the other types of ground and tremble for them. We are told that the wheat and the weeds are so intertwined that the latter cannot be removed without uprooting the former, and this is what we see in the Church today.[7] But we must be very clear that the harvest is coming, and that when it does, the weeds will be separated from the wheat and the judgement will be severe. We are warned in the New Testament of the dangers of falling away:

---

[6] Matthew 13:1–9; 13–18.
[7] Matthew 13:24–30.

> It is impossible, in the case of those who have once been enlightened, who have tasted the heavenly gift, and have shared in the Holy Spirit, and have tasted the goodness of the Word of God and the powers of the age to come, and then have fallen away, to restore them again to repentance, since they are crucifying once again the Son of God to their own harm and holding him up to contempt.[8]

We are called to work out our own salvation with fear and trembling.[9] Paul kept a constant guard over himself because he knew that it was all too possible that he might preach to others, only to find that he had not put his own message into practice and would have to suffer the consequences.[10] Orthodox Christians are blessed in that we have standards and safeguards to keep us on the straight and narrow path that leads to eternal life, but we must never despise or neglect the gift that God has given to us.[11]

Orthodoxy matters because it is the bedrock of assurance on which our faith is based. When we look at the 'progressives' and 'revisionists' around us, what do we see? We see people who are anxious that their message is not being heard, and may even think that they are being secretly sabotaged by their opponents. We see people who will resort to any means, fair or foul, to promote their cause. One of the saddest things about the recent controversies in the Anglican world

---

[8] Hebrews 6:4–6.
[9] Philippians 2:12.
[10] 1 Corinthians 9:27.
[11] 2 Timothy 1:6.

is the loss of confidence between the orthodox and the 'revisionists' caused by the latter's behaviour. The majority of Anglicans worldwide believe that they have been betrayed by the central instruments of the Anglican Communion. They say that they have been lied to by people who have promised to discipline the wanderers but who have then failed to do so. Even within the Church of England, trust between the House of Bishops and the rest of the Church is at an all-time low. The backtracking, obfuscation and gaslighting that has characterised the way the Living in Love and Faith process has been manipulated is such that nobody can believe a word that they have heard. The promises that there will be protections and safeguards for orthodox people are not believed, for the very good reason that so far none have been offered. The official line seems to be: 'Accept the revisionist position now and we shall take care of you later.' Later, unfortunately, never comes.

This matters, because deceit and dishonesty can never be the foundation of a healthy Church. Orthodox people know this, but how should we respond to the provocations that keep coming our way? Paul set down some principles in his letter to his disciple Titus. He said that we should be ready for every good work, speak evil of no one, avoid quarrelling, be gentle, and show perfect courtesy toward all people.[12] Unfortunately, there are some who claim to be orthodox who have not hesitated to ignore the apostle's advice and who have launched personal attacks on the Archbishop of Canterbury (in particular) as well as on others in the 'revisionist' camp. We should not be surprised by this. Paul was also provoked when he was trying to defend himself, and he attacked the Jewish high priest

---

[12] Titus 3:1–2.

without realising it. But when he was told what he had (inadvertently) done, he apologised, because it was against the law to speak evil of the ruler of the people.[13]

This is not the way. As Paul reminded Titus: 'We ourselves were once foolish, disobedient, led astray, slaves to various passions and pleasures, passing our days in malice and envy, hated by others and hating one another.'[14] If we treat our opponents in the way they treat us, they will have won the argument and our witness will be compromised, perhaps beyond repair. We must avoid this, and plead with our over-zealous brethren to consider their own spiritual condition and refrain from ungodly accusations against people with whom we disagree.

At the same time, we must continue to assert as best we can that orthodoxy matters, because those who have forsaken it are in grave danger of losing their souls. We are not at liberty to jettison the salvation that has been offered to us in Christ, even if we think it is in a good cause. Paul told the Romans that he would have acquiesced in his own damnation if it could have led to the redemption of his own Jewish people.[15] God would not let him make such a sacrifice, but the spirit in which he spoke is one that should move us all. Do we really care about 'revisionists'? Do we want to see them come to know Christ as their Lord and Saviour in the way we do, or do we secretly hope that they will be condemned by the just judgement of God? If we do not share Paul's anguish for those who have turned away from the faith once delivered to the saints, then what good is our witness? Cold orthodoxy is no more

---

[13] Acts 23:2–5; Exodus 22:28.
[14] Titus 3:3.
[15] Romans 9:3.

acceptable to God than heresy is – in fact, it is a form of heresy itself! Let Paul have the last word:

> When the goodness and loving kindness of God our Saviour appeared, he saved us, not because of works done by us in righteousness, but according to his own mercy, by the washing of regeneration and renewal of the Holy Spirit, whom he poured out on us richly through Jesus Christ our Saviour, so that being justified by his grace we might become heirs according to the hope of eternal life.[16]

There is orthodoxy summed up in a nutshell, where doctrine and practice go together and our lives are transformed. Let us pray that all who claim the name of Christ may come to know this in their own hearts and lives, so that the Church may be healed of its heresies and schisms, and the light of Christ may shine ever more brightly until the day when he comes again in his glory.

---

[16] Titus 3:4–7.

In our Christian Doctrine series

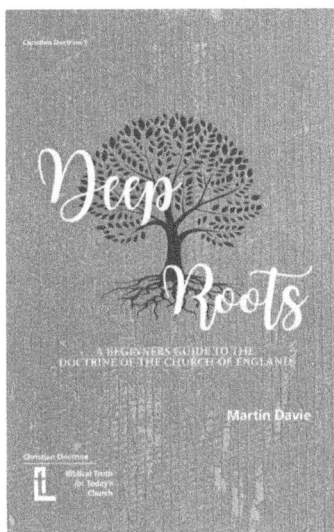

Those authorised to minister in the Church of England, whether as ordained or lay ministers, are expected to teach and act in accordance with the Church of England's doctrine. However, many of those who are currently exercising ministry in the Church of England, or who are being trained for ministry, are unclear about what the Church of England's doctrine is, and why it matters that they should adhere to it.

In order to address this situation, the Latimer Trust is producing a new series of short books on doctrine which are designed to introduce various key aspects of the doctrine of the Church of England. The purpose of *Deep Roots* is to introduce the series as a whole. It does this by explaining what doctrine is, the nature of the doctrinal authorities accepted by the Church of

England, and why it is important for both ministers (and Christians in general) to adhere to what is taught by these doctrinal authorities.

This is a book for existing ministers, those in training for ministry and ordinary lay Christians who want a concise but reliable answer to the question 'What is doctrine and why does it matter?'

In our Leadership series

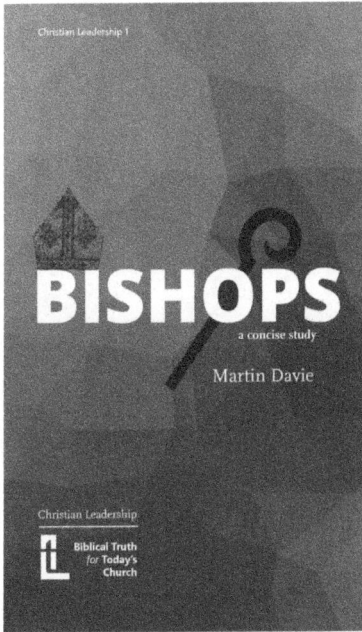

Bishops: A Concise Study summarises the key points of Martin Davie's major study *Bishops Past, Present and Future* (Gilead Books, 2022). It is designed to meet the needs of those who would like to know about the role and importance of bishops in the Church of England, but who would baulk at tackling the 800+ pages of the original book.

This concise study is published in the hope that it will help many in the Church of England, both ordained and lay, to think in a more informed fashion about how bishops should respond to the challenges and opportunities facing the Church of England at this critical point in its history.

Also published by the Latimer Trust:

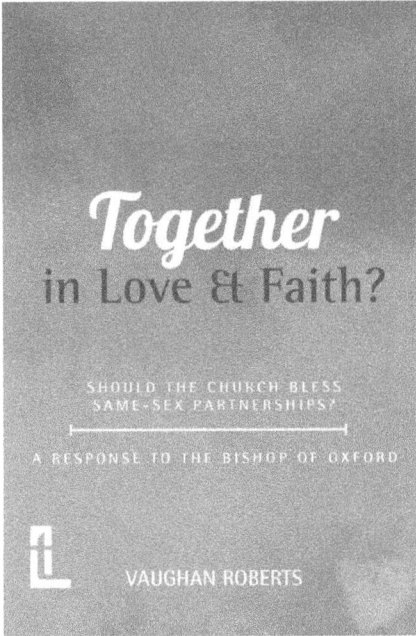

Together
in Love & Faith?

SHOULD THE CHURCH BLESS
SAME-SEX PARTNERSHIPS?

A RESPONSE TO THE BISHOP OF OXFORD

VAUGHAN ROBERTS

Writing from his own experience of same-sex attraction, Vaughan Roberts responds to the Bishop of Oxford's argument that the Church of England should change its doctrine and practice in relation to same-sex relationships. He outlines the beauty and goodness of the Bible's teaching on sex and marriage, as traditionally understood, and calls for it to be upheld with sensitivity and pastoral wisdom.

www.ingramcontent.com/pod-product-compliance
Lightning Source LLC
Chambersburg PA
CBHW021143020426
42331CB00005B/881